1•2•3
I Can Sculpt!

Irene Luxbacher

KIDS CAN PRESS

A sculpture is a piece of **ART** that has more than one side to look at. It can look like something real or something you imagine. Let's sculpt animals …

R0413142718

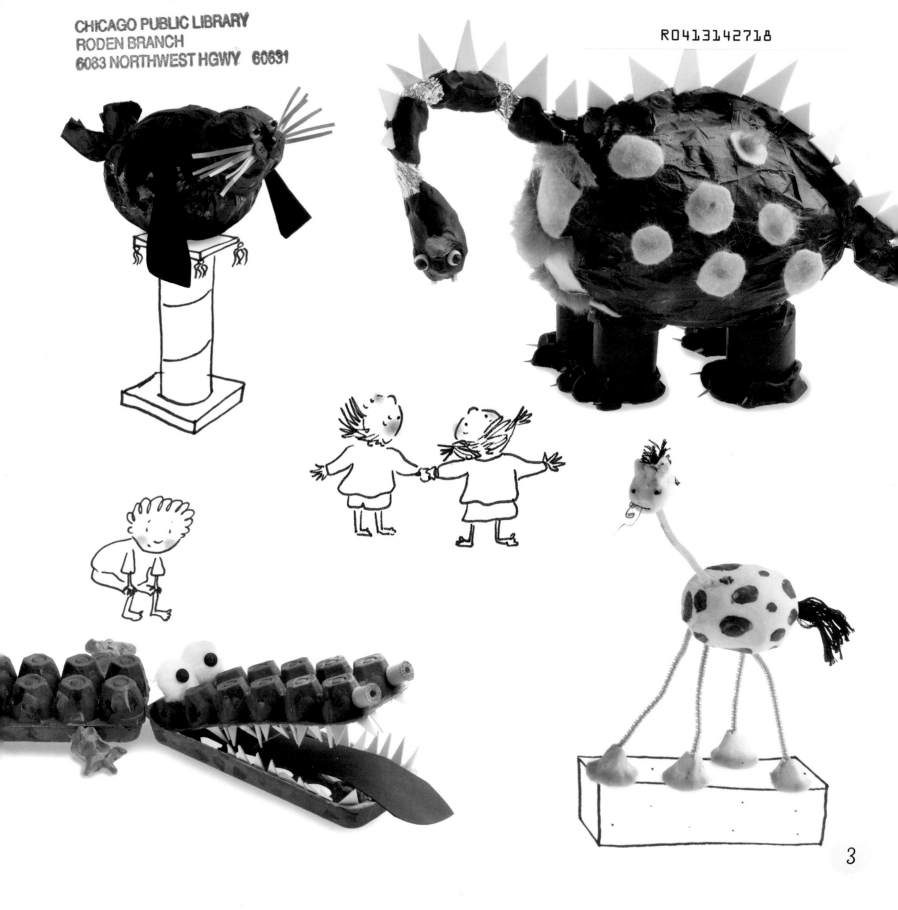

3

The things you use to
make a sculpture are called
MATERIALS.

- OLD NEWSPAPERS
(TO PROTECT YOUR
WORK SURFACE)

- PAINTS AND PAINTBRUSHES

- A SMOCK (TO PROTECT
YOUR CLOTHES)

- MODELING CLAY (LIKE
PLASTICINE OR PLAY DOUGH)

4

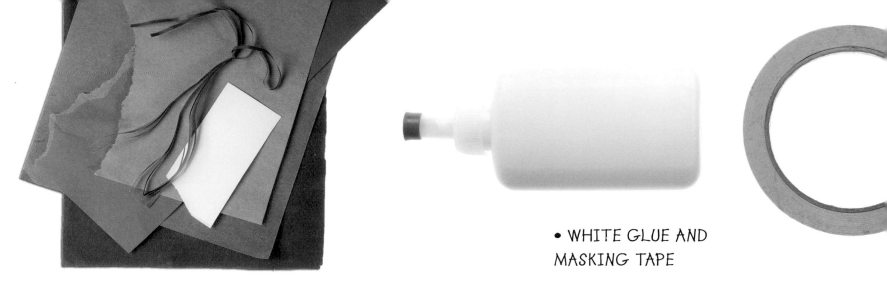

- SCRAPS OF FABRIC AND PAPER

- WHITE GLUE AND MASKING TAPE

- BEADS AND BUTTONS

- ALUMINUM FOIL

- PIPE CLEANERS

- EGG CARTONS AND CARDBOARD TUBES

FORMING an IDEA

What can you make out of two egg cartons, two cotton balls and two empty spools of thread? How about a *HUNGRY CROCODILE?*

1. Carefully cut along the fold of an egg carton. Make a crocodile's head with open jaws by taping the two pieces of carton together at one end. (You might need a helper to hold the pieces while you tape.) Paint the head green with a fat brush.

2. Glue two cotton ball eyes near the taped end of the crocodile's jaws. Next glue two spool nostrils near the open end.

3. Cut some triangle teeth out of construction paper or a sheet of craft foam. Glue them along the inside of your crocodile's jaws.

CHOMP, CHOMP!
A Toothy Crocodile!

Give your crocodile a body by lining up another painted egg carton. Next add four legs and a tail shaped out of modeling clay. Cut and place a red fabric or paper tongue inside the mouth. Glue a small button or bead to the center of each cotton ball eye. Now your croc is complete!

By putting different materials and shapes together to make your crocodile, you have made a **FORM**.

STUFF It

Making a sculpture is as easy as turning something FLAT into something FAT. Try it by turning an empty paper bag into a round sea lion!

1. Stuff a paper lunch bag with some scraps of paper or fabric. Twist the end closed, and tape it with masking tape to make your sea lion's back flippers. Wrap more tape tightly around part of the sea lion's body to make its neck and head.

2. Carefully cut or rip your tail up the middle. Then paint your sea lion using a fat brush. Let the paint dry.

3. Cut some construction paper into thin strips for whiskers and glue them to your sea lion's face. Cut two triangle flippers out of construction paper or craft foam. Glue one to each side of your sea lion's body.

SPLASH!
A Sunbathing Sea Lion!

Glue on beads and buttons for the nose and eyes. Set your sculpture on a handful of sand or a smooth rock. Or think of another place where your sunbathing sea lion would like to sit.

Your sea lion has more than one side to look at. It is 3-DIMENSIONAL. All sculptures are 3-dimensional.

9

Ins-s-side OUT

Sometimes the INSIDE of a sculpture is as important as the OUTSIDE. A skeleton made with twisted aluminum foil helps this skinny snake keep its shape.

1. Twist three long sheets of aluminum foil into snakelike pieces. Then twist the ends of the pieces together tightly to make one long snake.

2. Bend your snake's skeleton into some silly twists and curves.

3. Flatten some pieces of modeling clay between your hands to make your snake's skin. Wrap and press the flattened clay over the skeleton a piece at a time, covering it as much as you want.

10

S-S-S-S! A Silly Snake!

Decorate your snake with colorful stripes, spots and scales made of pressed-on bits of modeling clay. Roll out a small clay head and press it onto one end of your snake. Press in beads or buttons for eyes. S-s-super s-s-sculpture!

The skeleton inside a sculpture is called an **ARMATURE** (say *arm-a-cher*).

ROLL, PRESS, PINCH, POKE

Modeling clay is a fun material for making all sorts of sculptures. Roll, press, pinch and poke a lump of Plasticine or play dough into a whole *FLOCK OF BIRDS!*

1. Take a piece of modeling clay about the size of your palm and another about the size of a marble. Roll each piece into a ball. Press the balls together to make your bird's body and head.

2. Take another piece of modeling clay about the size of your palm and press it until it's as flat as a pancake. Use scissors to carefully cut out two triangles and press them onto the bird's body for its wings.

3. Pinch a pointy beak out of the head. Then use the tip of a pencil to poke in two eyes. To make a colorful tail, press a few feathers or strips of curled construction paper into the bird's body.

SQUAWK! A Whole Flock!

Give your bird sculpture a nice, high perch.
First press a big lump of modeling clay
onto your work surface for a base.
Then poke one end of a
chopstick into the
base, and poke the
other end into the
bottom of your bird.
Sculpt a few more birds,
and you've got a flock of
feathered friends!

Artists use special
TECHNIQUES
to make art.
ROLLING,
PRESSING,
PINCHING
and POKING
are techniques for
working with
modeling clay.

13

TOUCHY, TOUCHY

Some sculptures are made to be TOUCHED! Use an old sock and some cotton balls to make a sculpture that's as SOFT as a little lamb.

1. Stuff fabric scraps into an old sock to make your lamb's body. Tie the open end of the sock closed with a pipe cleaner or twist tie.

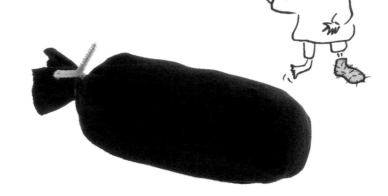

2. One at a time, dip one end of each cotton ball into white glue and press them onto the stuffed sock. Cover most of your lamb's body, but leave a little space at the untied end so your lamb's face can peek through. Let the glue dry.

3. Roll four pieces of modeling clay into thick little legs about the size of marshmallows. Set your woolly lamb's body on top of the legs.

BAAA!
A Soft Little Lamb!

Glue small beads on your lamb's face for eyes and a nose. Glue on a tiny red paper or fabric mouth. Cut two floppy ears out of a scrap of soft fabric. Glue an ear on either side of its face. Glue a cotton ball tail to the tied end of your lamb's body. What a lovely little lamb!

The way something feels when you TOUCH it is called TEXTURE. What other textures can you think of besides "soft"?

KEEPING Your BALANCE

When you stand on one foot, it's easy to lose your balance and fall over. Your sculpture of a giraffe will keep its balance by having all four of its feet on the ground.

1. To make the body, take a piece of modeling clay about the size of your palm and roll it into a ball. Poke four pipe cleaners into the body for legs that are all the same length. Poke another pipe cleaner into the body for your giraffe's long neck.

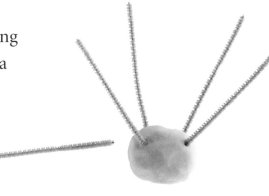

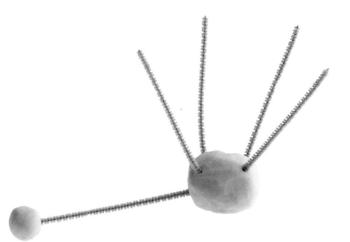

2. Roll a piece of modeling clay about the size of your thumb into a ball, and press it onto the end of your giraffe's neck to make the head.

3. Roll four small balls of modeling clay and press one onto the end of each leg. Stand your giraffe up, pressing the clay feet down a bit onto your work surface. If your giraffe has trouble standing, try moving its body until you find the right balance.

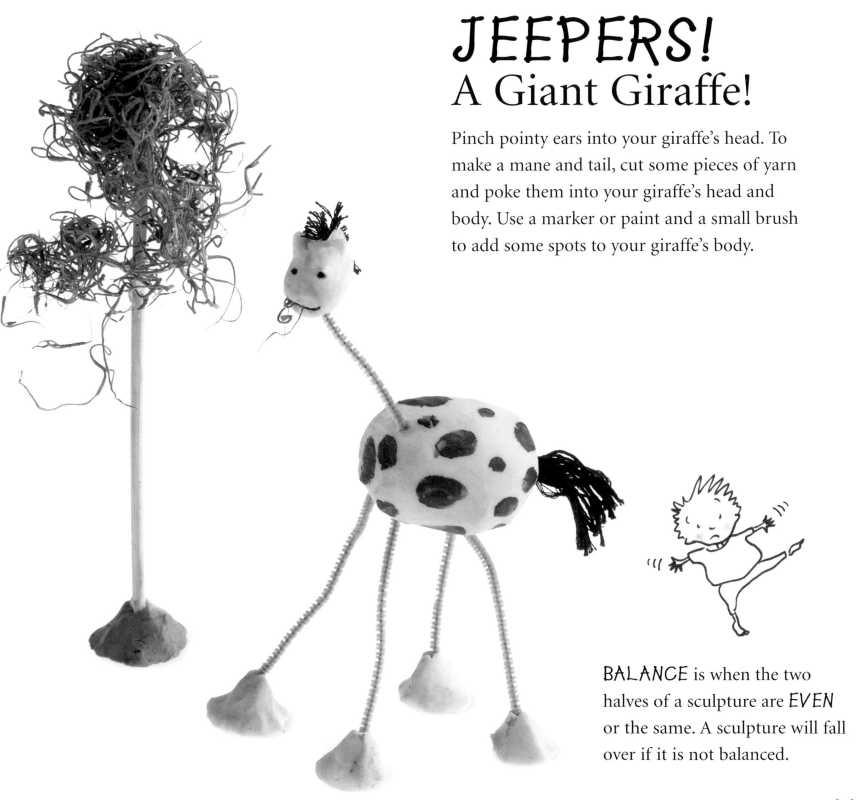

JEEPERS!
A Giant Giraffe!

Pinch pointy ears into your giraffe's head. To make a mane and tail, cut some pieces of yarn and poke them into your giraffe's head and body. Use a marker or paint and a small brush to add some spots to your giraffe's body.

BALANCE is when the two halves of a sculpture are EVEN or the same. A sculpture will fall over if it is not balanced.

17

Do-It-Yourself DINO

What can you make if you take steps from all
your animal sculptures and put them together?
A sculpture of a dinosaur! *ROAR!*

DINOSAUR PARTS

Gather up what you'll need to make your dinosaur's
form: a paper lunch bag, scraps of paper or fabric,
aluminum foil and empty toilet paper rolls. You'll
also use modeling clay, fun fur, beads, craft foam
and colorful paints to decorate your dinosaur.

BODY

Stuff a paper lunch bag with some
scraps of paper or fabric. Twist the end
closed, and tape it with masking tape.

NECK AND TAIL

Twist three sheets of aluminum foil
into a snakelike shape. Twist the ends
of the pieces together tightly to make
one long piece. Tape it down the
middle of your dinosaur's paper bag
body so its ends make a neck and tail.

SKIN

Roll a thumb-sized head out of modeling clay, and stick it onto the end of your dino's neck. Add some dino skin by pressing flattened pieces of modeling clay over the neck and tail. Paint your dinosaur's paper bag body and let dry.

FUR

Add some furry texture by cutting strips and circles out of scraps of fun fur or fuzzy fabric and gluing them onto your dinosaur.

LEGS

Ask an adult to cut two toilet paper rolls in half to make four legs. Press a palm-sized piece of flattened modeling clay onto each end of the legs. Stand the legs up, and sit the body on top. Play with the position of the legs and body until your dino keeps its balance. Glue the body to the legs with white glue. Let the glue dry.

19

WOW-a-saurus!

Paint your dinosaur's legs, and let them dry. Cut small triangles out of craft foam, and glue them in a line down your dinosaur's neck, back and tail. Add more finishing touches like beads for eyes and toes pinched out of the feet.

Putting your sculpture
next to a smaller
sculpture or toy will
make it seem bigger.

21

Note to PARENTS and TEACHERS

We chose animals as a fun theme for exploring some basic sculpting techniques, but there are lots of other topics or themes you can use to inspire your young artist. Here are a few ideas to get you started.

• Make a sculpture of a mini solar system. Start with stuffed paper bag forms for planets and moons (see Stuff It, pages 8–9). Add pinched and pressed stars made with pieces of colorful clay or Plasticine (see Roll, Press, Pinch, Poke, pages 12–13). Sculpt some alien life forms using pipe cleaners and bits of clay (see Keeping Your Balance, pages 16–17).

• Or make a soft, squishy caterpillar. Stuff a long sock (see Touchy, Touchy, pages 14–15) for the caterpillar's body. Use aluminum foil and Plasticine (see Ins-s-side Out, pages 10–11) to add long, curly antennae and lots of fat legs to your caterpillar.

Tips to ensure a GREAT SCULPTING EXPERIENCE every time:

1. Use inexpensive materials and make sure your young artist's clothes and the work area are protected. This way it's all about the fun, not the waste or the mess.

2. Focus on the process rather than the end product. Make sure your young artist is relaxed and having fun with the information instead of expecting perfection every time.

3. Remind your young artist that mistakes are an artist's best friend. The most interesting sculpting techniques or ideas are often discovered by mistake.

22

ART Words

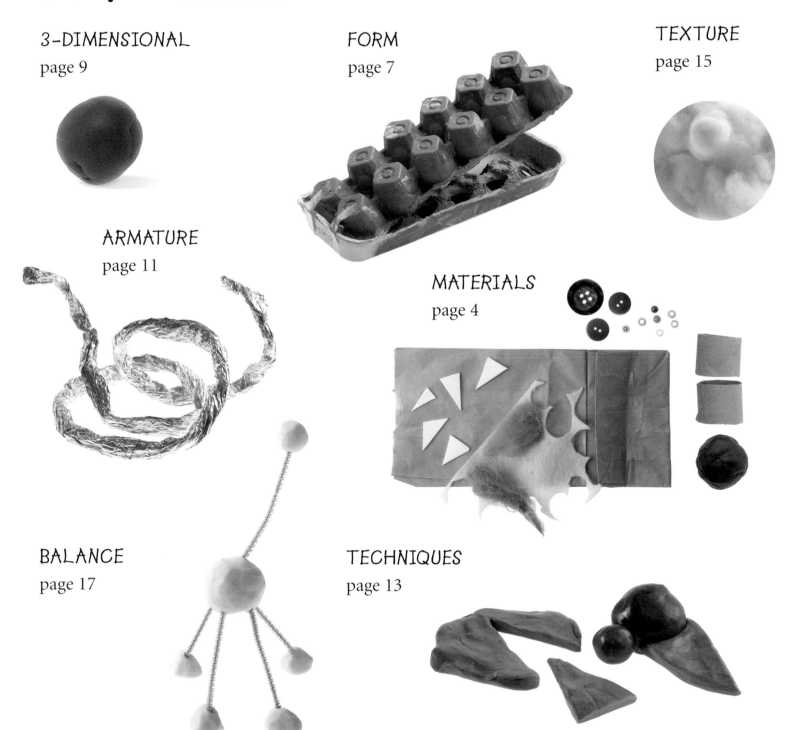

3-DIMENSIONAL
page 9

FORM
page 7

TEXTURE
page 15

ARMATURE
page 11

MATERIALS
page 4

BALANCE
page 17

TECHNIQUES
page 13

23

FOR MY FAMILY: FRANK, SOPHIA, NICK, LESLIE AND ELIJAH

Many thanks to Valerie Hussey for her encouragement, and special thanks to Stacey Roderick and Karen Powers for their amazing talents and insights on this project.

Kids Can Press acknowledges the financial support of the Government of Ontario, through the Ontario Media Development Corporation's Ontario Book Initiative, and the Government of Canada, through the BPIDP, for our publishing activity.

Published in Canada by
Kids Can Press Ltd.
29 Birch Avenue
Toronto, ON M4V 1E2

Published in the U.S. by
Kids Can Press Ltd.
2250 Military Road
Tonawanda, NY 14150

www.kidscanpress.com

Edited by Stacey Roderick
Designed by Karen Powers
Printed and bound in Singapore

The hardcover edition of this book is smyth sewn casebound.
The paperback edition of this book is limp sewn with a drawn-on cover.

CM 07 0 9 8 7 6 5 4 3 2 1
CM PA 07 0 9 8 7 6 5 4 3 2 1

Library and Archives Canada Cataloguing in Publication

Luxbacher, Irene, 1970–
    123 I can sculpt / written and illustrated by
Irene Luxbacher.

(Starting art)
ISBN 978-1-55453-038-0 (bound)
ISBN 978-1-55453-151-6 (pbk.)

1. Sculpture—Technique—Juvenile literature. I. Title.
II. Title: One, two, three I can sculpt. III. Series.

NB1170.L89 2007   j731.4   C2007-900201-3

Kids Can Press is a **corus**™ Entertainment company